JACKI PASSMORE

Thai

Photography by SIMON WHEELER

THE MASTER CHEFS

TED SMART

JACKI PASSMORE is the author of over 20 Asian cookbooks, including the award-winning *Asia the Beautiful Cookbook* and *The Encyclopedia of Asian Food and Cooking*. For 12 years she worked as a food writer in Hong Kong, travelling extensively to study the cuisines of Asia.

She now lives in Brisbane, Australia, with her daughter Isobel and a cat named Noodles. She continues her career as a food writer and restaurant consultant, and runs her cooking school, Jacki Passmore Cooks.

CONTENTS

To learn to cook, you have to learn to eat.

CHEONG LIEW

INTRODUCTION

Thai food is a particular passion for me. It's a love affair that long precedes my first visit there, beginning when I was given a cookbook entitled *Everyday Siamese Dishes*, written by Princess Sibpan Sonakul in the early 1960s. Here, in a modest paperback, was Thai royal cuisine side by side with everyday fare. Each dish told of flavours as vivid and exciting as Thailand itself. From our home in Hong Kong, we began to vacation in Thailand three or four times a year, each trip a voyage of fascinating discovery.

These ten recipes encapsulate Thai cuisine as it unfolded for me. The fish in ginger sauce was my very first meal there, in the legendary Oriental Hotel in Bangkok. Tom Yam hot and sour soup and the hot and spicy pork with beans taught me just how hot a chilli can be. I learnt from Mussaman curry that Indian spice traders had their input in Thai cooking centuries ago, and from the Laab Kai that so too had the Laotians and Vietnamese. I can't eat Kai Yang without remembering trips north to Chiang Mai, or Pad Thai without recalling al fresco meals in Thai night markets. Thai food is hot. It's often pungent. But it's never, never dull!

Jacki Passmore

CHICKEN AND HERB SALAD
(Laab Kai)

450 G/1 LB BONELESS, SKINLESS
    CHICKEN BREAST
2 SMALL CUCUMBERS
1 ONION
1 RED ONION
6 CHIVES OR GARLIC CHIVES,
    SNIPPED
SMALL BUNCH OF MINT
SMALL BUNCH OF CORIANDER
SMALL BUNCH OF BASIL
1½ TABLESPOONS THAI FISH
    SAUCE
2 TABLESPOONS LIME JUICE
1 TABLESPOON SWEET CHILLI SAUCE
1–2 GARLIC CLOVES, FINELY
    CHOPPED
2½ TEASPOONS SUGAR

SERVES 4

Cut the chicken into 1 cm/½ inch cubes. Heat a nonstick pan and cook the chicken – without adding any oil – for about 3 minutes, shaking the pan and stirring frequently. As soon as the chicken is cooked through, remove from the heat and set aside to cool.

Cut the cucumbers in half lengthways, scoop out and discard the seeds, and slice thinly. Cut the onions in half and slice thinly. Place the cucumber, onions and chives in a salad bowl and toss gently to combine.

Pick off the mint, coriander and basil leaves, reserving a few sprigs for garnish. Add the leaves to the salad.

Put the remaining ingredients in a bowl and whisk together to make the dressing. Add the chicken and mix well, then add to the salad and toss gently to combine. Serve garnished with the reserved herbs.

FRIED FISH CAKES
(Tod Mun Pla)

2 SLICES OF FRESH GINGER

1–2 GARLIC CLOVES

1 SPRING ONION, CHOPPED

2 TABLESPOONS CHOPPED FRESH
LEMON GRASS

325 G/12 OZ BONELESS, SKINLESS
WHITE FISH (COD, LING),
CUT INTO CUBES

1 TABLESPOON THAI FISH SAUCE

1 EGG

1 TEASPOON SALT

½ TEASPOON GROUND PEPPER

1½ SNAKE/LONG BEANS OR
4 GREEN BEANS

VEGETABLE OIL FOR DEEP-FRYING

CUCUMBER SAUCE (PAGE 29)

SERVES 4

Place the ginger, garlic, spring onion and lemon grass in a food processor and process to a paste.

Add the fish to the food processor. Using the pulse control, chop for about 1 minute, then add the fish sauce, egg, salt, pepper and 2 tablespoons of cold water and process until you have a smooth, thick purée.

Cut the beans into paper-thin slices and add to the fish purée. Process just long enough for them to be incorporated. (If the beans are not cut paper-thin, they should be briefly parboiled and well drained before adding to the fish.)

Heat the oil in a wok or deep frying pan to 180–190°C/ 350–375°F or until a cube of bread browns in 30 seconds. Drop heaped teaspoons of the fish purée into the oil, about eight at a time. Fry until they float to the surface, then turn and cook until golden brown on both sides, about 1–2 minutes. Drain on paper towels and serve at once, with the cucumber sauce for dipping.

HOT AND SOUR PRAWN SOUP
(Tom Yam Gung)

16 RAW PRAWNS, IN THEIR SHELLS

1 LEMON GRASS STALK, SLIT
  LENGTHWAYS

8 THIN SLICES OF FRESH GINGER

1 FISH STOCK CUBE OR 1 TOM YAM
  BROTH CUBE

2 FRESH RED CHILLIES, SEEDED AND
  CUT IN HALF

2 KAFFIR LIME LEAVES, OR 4 STRIPS
  OF LIME PEEL

1 TOMATO, CUT INTO WEDGES

2 TABLESPOONS THAI FISH SAUCE

SALT AND PEPPER

SMALL BUNCH OF CORIANDER

2–3 LIMES

SERVES 4

Place the prawns in a saucepan
with 1.5 litres/2½ pints water. Add
the lemon grass, ginger and stock
cube. Bring to the boil and simmer
for 1 minute. Remove and shell
the prawns.

Return the prawn shells to the
stock with the chillies and lime
leaves or peel. Simmer for 5–6
minutes, then strain the stock into
a clean saucepan. Retrieve the
chillies and lime leaves (discard the
peel and lemon grass) and return
to the strained stock.

Add the tomato to the stock
and simmer for 2–3 minutes.

Season the soup with fish sauce,
salt and pepper. Add the coriander
leaves, squeeze in the juice of two
limes and drop in the lime skins.
You are aiming for a taste that is
hot and sour with a distinct citrus
flavour. Adjust the flavour to your
taste with additional lime juice or a
pinch of salt.

Return the prawns to the soup
to heat through, then serve at once.

GINGER FISH
(Pla Prio Wan)

1 WHOLE SNAPPER OR SEA BREAM,
   ABOUT 675 G/1½ LB,
   CLEANED AND SCALED
SALT AND WHITE PEPPER
2–3 TABLESPOONS CORNFLOUR
600 ML/1 PINT VEGETABLE OIL
8 DRIED CHINESE MUSHROOMS,
   SOAKED FOR 25 MINUTES
2 SPRING ONIONS, SHREDDED
1 TABLESPOON THAI FISH SAUCE OR
   LIGHT SOY SAUCE
2 TABLESPOONS DARK SOY SAUCE
50 G/2 OZ SOFT BROWN SUGAR
85 G/3 OZ PICKLED GINGER,
   SHREDDED
4 TABLESPOONS LIQUID FROM THE
   PICKLED GINGER
175 ML/6 FL OZ WATER
1–2 TEASPOONS LIME JUICE
CORIANDER SPRIGS AND EXTRA
   PICKLED GINGER, TO GARNISH

SERVES 4

Using a sharp knife, make several deep slashes across each side of the fish. Season lightly with salt and pepper, then coat with cornflour, reserving 3 teaspoons.

Heat the oil in a wok or large frying pan to 180–190°C/ 350–375°F or until a cube of bread browns in 30 seconds. Carefully slide in the fish and fry for about 2½ minutes on each side. Remove and set aside on a plate, covered with foil.

Drain the mushrooms, cut off the stems and slice the caps finely. Heat 1½ tablespoons oil in a small saucepan. Sauté the mushrooms and spring onions for 1 minute, then add the fish sauce and soy sauce, sugar, pickled ginger and its liquid, and bring back to the boil.

Blend the reserved cornflour with the water. Pour into the saucepan and stir over medium-high heat until the sauce thickens.

Place the fish on a platter and spoon the sauce over. Garnish with coriander sprigs and ginger. Serve with boiled or fried rice.

GRILLED PEPPER CHICKEN WITH SPICED PEANUT SAUCE (Kai Yang)

8 CHICKEN THIGHS (SKINNED IF
  PREFERRED)
2 TABLESPOONS PEANUT OR
  VEGETABLE OIL
2–3 GARLIC CLOVES, CRUSHED
1½ TABLESPOONS THAI FISH
  SAUCE OR LIGHT SOY SAUCE
1 TABLESPOON VERY FINELY
  CHOPPED FRESH CORIANDER
  (OPTIONAL)
1 TEASPOON SALT
1 TABLESPOON COARSELY GROUND
  WHITE PEPPER
275 G/10 OZ CHINESE CABBAGE,
  COARSELY CHOPPED
2 TEASPOONS FINELY GRATED
  FRESH GINGER
SPICED PEANUT SAUCE (PAGE 29)

SERVES 4

Using a fork, prick the skin of the chicken all over, to allow the flavours to penetrate. Brush with a little of the oil. Grind together the garlic, fish sauce or soy sauce, coriander, salt and pepper to form a paste. Spread over the chicken and set aside for at least 1 hour.

Heat the grill to moderate and cook the chicken, turning frequently, until golden brown and cooked through, about 25 minutes.

Meanwhile, heat 1 tablespoon of the oil in a wok or large frying pan and stir-fry the cabbage with the ginger for about 5 minutes, then cover and cook gently until it is tender. Season to taste with salt and pepper.

Serve the cabbage on a large platter or individual plates. Place the chicken on the cabbage and spoon the peanut sauce over.

RED DUCK CURRY
(Gaeng Ped Bet)

1 DUCK, ABOUT 1.5 KG/3 LB

1 TABLESPOON VEGETABLE OR
   PEANUT OIL

1 ONION, CHOPPED

2 GARLIC CLOVES, CHOPPED

½ RECIPE THAI RED CURRY
   PASTE (PAGE 28)

375 ML/12 FL OZ COCONUT
   CREAM

250 ML/8 FL OZ WATER

2 FRESH RED CHILLIES, SEEDED

1 TEASPOON PAPRIKA

2 TEASPOONS SOFT BROWN SUGAR

SALT AND PEPPER

THAI FISH SAUCE

12 CHERRY TOMATOES

SMALL BUNCH OF BASIL LEAVES

SERVES 4–6

Cut the duck into small pieces.
Heat the oil in a large, heavy frying
pan over medium-high heat.
Brown the duck in the oil, turning
frequently so it colours evenly.
Remove excess fat with a spoon
and discard, or reserve for use
when stir-frying another dish.
Remove the duck and set aside.

In the same pan, brown the
onion and garlic for 3–4 minutes,
stirring frequently. Stir in the curry
paste and fry for 1–2 minutes, then
add the coconut cream and water,
the chillies, paprika and brown
sugar. Bring to the boil, then
reduce the heat and simmer for
6–8 minutes.

Return the duck to the pan
and simmer gently until the duck
is tender, about 40 minutes.

Taste and adjust the seasoning,
adding salt, pepper and fish sauce if
necessary. Add the cherry tomatoes
and basil and heat through. Serve
with boiled or steamed white rice.

MUSSAMAN BEEF CURRY
(Gaeng Mussaman)

600 G/1¼ LB BEEF SHIN OR
    OTHER BRAISING STEAK

2½ TABLESPOONS VEGETABLE OR
    PEANUT OIL

3 ONIONS, CHOPPED

3 GARLIC CLOVES, CHOPPED

2 CM/¾ INCH PIECE OF FRESH
    GINGER, GRATED OR CHOPPED

1 LEMON GRASS STALK, SLIT
    LENGTHWAYS

1 SMALL FRESH RED CHILLI, SEEDED

2 TABLESPOONS GROUND
    CORIANDER

2 TEASPOONS GROUND CUMIN

2 WHOLE CLOVES

1 SMALL CINNAMON STICK

2 POINTS STAR ANISE (OPTIONAL)

2½ TEASPOONS SOFT BROWN
    SUGAR

500 ML/16 FL OZ COCONUT
    CREAM

125 ML/4 FL OZ WATER

3 POTATOES, CUBED

SALT AND PEPPER

THAI FISH SAUCE (OPTIONAL)

LIME JUICE (OPTIONAL)

50 G/2 OZ ROASTED PEANUTS,
    ROUGHLY CHOPPED

SERVES 4–6

Cut the beef into 4 cm/1½ inch cubes. Heat the oil in a saucepan over medium heat and brown the onions for about 6 minutes.

Add the garlic, ginger and lemon grass and cook for 2 minutes. Add the chilli, all the spices and the sugar, with 375 ml/ 12 fl oz of the coconut cream and the water, and bring to just below boiling point.

Add the beef and cover the pan. Cook for about 55 minutes, stirring the meat occasionally.

Pour in the remaining coconut cream and add the potatoes, salt and pepper. Cook for a further 20 minutes or until the potatoes are tender. Taste and adjust the seasoning, adding more salt and pepper and a splash of Thai fish sauce or lime juice if you like. Stir in the peanuts and serve with boiled or steamed white rice.

HOT AND SPICY PORK WITH BEANS (*Pad Prik King Tua Fak Yaeow*)

400 G/14 OZ LEAN PORK

1½ TABLESPOONS VEGETABLE OIL

2 SPRING ONIONS, SHREDDED

1 TABLESPOON FINELY SHREDDED
    FRESH GINGER

1 TABLESPOON CHOPPED GARLIC

2 FRESH RED CHILLIES, SEEDED

½ RECIPE THAI RED CURRY
    PASTE (PAGE 28)

1 TEASPOON SHRIMP PASTE

1 TEASPOON PAPRIKA

125 ML/4 FL OZ COCONUT CREAM

1 TEASPOON SUGAR

125 ML/4 FL OZ WATER

4–5 SNAKE/LONG BEANS OR
    12 GREEN BEANS, CUT INTO
    5 CM/2 INCH PIECES

½ RED PEPPER, CUT INTO STRIPS

SALT

SERVES 4

Cut the pork into thin strips and set aside.

Heat the oil in a wok or large heavy frying pan and stir-fry the spring onions, ginger, garlic and chillies for about 1½ minutes. Add the curry paste, shrimp paste and paprika and stir-fry for 1 minute.

Add the strips of pork, coconut cream and sugar and stir-fry over high heat until the liquid has been absorbed. Add the water and the beans and continue to cook, stirring frequently, until the beans are tender.

Add the strips of pepper and salt to taste. Cook, stirring frequently, until the liquid has been absorbed and the meat and vegetables are tender. Serve with boiled rice or rice noodles.

THAI NOODLES
(Pad Thai)

300–325 G/11–12 OZ RICE STICKS
  (FLAT RICE NOODLES)
2–2½ TABLESPOONS VEGETABLE
  OR PEANUT OIL
1 ONION, FINELY SLICED
2 GARLIC CLOVES, SLICED
175 G/6 OZ BONELESS, SKINLESS
  CHICKEN BREAST
150 G/5 OZ SMALL PEELED PRAWNS
2–3 SPRING ONIONS, CHOPPED
175 G/6 OZ FRESH BEANSPROUTS
3–4 TABLESPOONS THAI FISH SAUCE
SALT AND PEPPER
2–3 TABLESPOONS ROASTED
  PEANUTS, CHOPPED
1 FRESH RED CHILLI, SEEDED AND
  FINELY SHREDDED (OPTIONAL)
LIME WEDGES, TO GARNISH

SERVES 4

Bring a large saucepan of water to the boil and add the noodles. Cook for about 3 minutes, until just tender, but still firm to the bite, then drain and set aside.

Heat the oil in a wok or large frying pan. Sauté the onion and garlic until lightly browned, about 4 minutes.

Cut the chicken into 1 cm/ ½ inch cubes. Push the onion to the side of the pan, add the chicken and stir-fry until evenly browned, then add the prawns, spring onions and beansprouts and cook over high heat for about 2½ minutes, stirring constantly.

Add the drained noodles and stir-fry until heated through, keeping them moving to prevent sticking. Season to taste with fish sauce, salt and pepper.

Serve on a large platter or individual plates and scatter over the peanuts and shredded chilli, if using. Garnish with lime wedges for squeezing.

BAKED COCONUT CUSTARD
(Songkaya)

375 ML/12 FL OZ COCONUT
CREAM
5 LARGE EGGS
125 G/4 OZ SOFT BROWN SUGAR
40 G/1½ OZ DESICCATED
COCONUT

SERVES 6–8

Preheat the oven to 180°C/350°F/
Gas Mark 4. Butter a 1.2 litre/
2 pint ovenproof dish.

Combine the coconut cream,
eggs, sugar and coconut in a large
bowl and place over a saucepan of
simmering water. Cook over
medium heat, whisking constantly,
for about 10 minutes or until the
custard has begun to thicken.

Pour the custard into the
buttered dish and place the dish in
a bain-marie or deep roasting tin.
Pour in warm water to come
halfway up the sides of the dish.
Place in the preheated oven for
about 45 minutes or until the
custard is set.

To serve warm, sprinkle the
surface with brown sugar and glaze
under a hot grill. Serve with
whipped cream. To serve cold,
accompany the custard with
poached fruit or a fruit compote.

THE BASICS

RED CURRY PASTE

10 DRIED RED CHILLIES, SOAKED
   FOR 20 MINUTES
6 GARLIC CLOVES
1 LEMON GRASS STALK, CHOPPED
2 SPRING ONIONS (WHITE PARTS),
   CHOPPED
2 CORIANDER SPRIGS (STEMS AND
   ROOTS ONLY), CHOPPED
1 TABLESPOON CHOPPED GALANGAL
   OR FRESH GINGER
1 TEASPOON GRATED LIME ZEST
1 TEASPOON PEPPERCORNS
½ TEASPOON GROUND CUMIN
1 TEASPOON SALT
1 TEASPOON SHRIMP PASTE
2–3 TABLESPOONS VEGETABLE OR
   PEANUT OIL

**THE EQUIVALENT OF
8 TEASPOONS OF
COMMERCIAL RED CURRY
PASTE**
Grind all the ingredients together
in a food processor, blender or
spice grinder, to form a reasonably
smooth paste.

   If you wish to keep the paste
for more than 3 days, fry in a
nonstick pan for about 6 minutes
over medium heat, stirring
frequently. Cool and store in a
covered glass jar.

CUCUMBER SAUCE

1 SMALL CUCUMBER (ABOUT 85 G/
   3 OZ), VERY FINELY DICED
1½ TABLESPOONS VERY FINELY
   CHOPPED SPRING ONION
1 SMALL RED CHILLI, SEEDED AND
   VERY FINELY CHOPPED
85 ML/3 FL OZ WHITE VINEGAR
85 ML/3 FL OZ WATER
65 G/2½ OZ SUGAR
2 GARLIC CLOVES, SLICED
2-3 SLICES OF FRESH GINGER
PINCH OF SALT

Place the cucumber, spring onion and chilli in a glass or stainless steel bowl. In a small saucepan, boil the remaining ingredients for 2–3 minutes. Remove from the heat and leave to cool to room temperature, then strain over the cucumber mixture, discarding the garlic and ginger.

The sauce will keep for 4–5 days in the refrigerator.

SPICED PEANUT SAUCE

5 TABLESPOONS CRUNCHY PEANUT
   BUTTER
85 ML/3 FL OZ COCONUT CREAM
125 ML/4 FL OZ WATER
½–1 TEASPOON CHILLI SAUCE OR
   CHILLI PASTE
1 TABLESPOON THAI FISH SAUCE OR
   LIGHT SOY SAUCE
½ TEASPOON THAI RED CURRY
   PASTE OR 1 TEASPOON MILD
   CURRY POWDER

¾ TEASPOON PALM SUGAR OR SOFT
   BROWN SUGAR
SALT AND PEPPER

Place all the ingredients in a small saucepan and stir over medium heat until thickened. Season to taste with salt and pepper.

INGREDIENTS

COCONUT CREAM

If canned coconut cream is not available, 4 tablespoons powdered coconut milk or creamed coconut block and 175 ml/6 fl oz water is the equivalent of 250 ml/8 fl oz coconut cream.

LEMON GRASS

1 teaspoon lemon grass powder or 1 teaspoon dried chopped lemon grass is the equivalent of 1 tablespoon chopped fresh lemon grass. Soak dried lemon grass in warm water for 20 minutes before use.

FISH SAUCE

Thai and Vietnamese fish sauce are the same. ½ teaspoon soft Chinese shrimp paste or 1 teaspoon anchovy essence could be substituted for 1 tablespoon fish sauce.

THE MASTER CHEFS

SOUPS
ARABELLA BOXER

MEZE, TAPAS AND ANTIPASTI
AGLAIA KREMEZI

PASTA SAUCES
GORDON RAMSAY

RISOTTO
MICHELE SCICOLONE

SALADS
CLARE CONNERY

MEDITERRANEAN
ANTONY WORRALL THOMPSON

VEGETABLES
PAUL GAYLER

LUNCHES
ALASTAIR LITTLE

COOKING FOR TWO
RICHARD OLNEY

FISH
RICK STEIN

CHICKEN
BRUNO LOUBET

SUPPERS
VALENTINA HARRIS

THE MAIN COURSE
ROGER VERGÉ

ROASTS
JANEEN SARLIN

WILD FOOD
ROWLEY LEIGH

PACIFIC
JILL DUPLEIX

CURRIES
PAT CHAPMAN

HOT AND SPICY
PAUL AND JEANNE RANKIN

THAI
JACKI PASSMORE

CHINESE
YAN-KIT SO

VEGETARIAN
KAREN LEE

DESSERTS
MICHEL ROUX

CAKES
CAROLE WALTER

COOKIES
ELINOR KLIVANS

THE MASTER CHEFS

This edition produced for The Book People Ltd,

Hall Wood Avenue, Haydock, St Helens WAII 9UL

Text © copyright 1996 Jacki Passmore

Jacki Passmore has asserted her right to be
identified as the Author of this Work.

Photographs © copyright 1996 Simon Wheeler

First published in 1996 by

WEIDENFELD & NICOLSON

THE ORION PUBLISHING GROUP

ORION HOUSE

5 UPPER ST MARTIN'S LANE

LONDON WC2H 9EA

British Library Cataloguing-in-Publication data
A catalogue record for this book is available
from the British Library.

ISBN 0 297 83644 7

DESIGNED BY THE SENATE

EDITOR MAGGIE RAMSAY

FOOD STYLIST JOY DAVIES